One thing Jeff Dunn will never have to worry about is his ability to communicate with grace, humor, and insight. As he focuses on "the everyday worry and anxiety that seek to rob our souls of life little by little," he stands with us as a friend in our fearfulness and helps us find a bit of peace and encouragement in God's loving and active presence.

CHAPLAIN MIKE MERCER,
author of Walking Home Together: Spiritual Guidance & Practical Advice for the End of Life

Why Worry, by Jeff Dunn, is a wise, kindly, and encouraging book. Jeff's own insights are enriched by the lives and words of saints and authors who have plunged through the pounding waves of worry and learned to float. Anyone who has ever worried—and that's all of us—will benefit by reading this book.

DARARIS ZEHNER, *author of The Between Time: Savoring the Sacred Moments of Everyday Life*

A quick look around gives us plenty of reasons to worry. Whether it's financial insecurity, a troubled relationship, precarious health, or growing unrest in the world, our temptation is to surrender to anxiety and be paralyzed by fear. In the pages of his new book, Jeff Dunn, a seasoned worrier himself, reminds us—through stories in Scripture, through the lives of saints who faced every trouble we face, and through the promises and provisions of our loving Father—precisely what is true. Faith, not worry, is the grace-filled, God-pleasing, surprisingly sane, and completely possible response of those who want to live in Christ.

LISA DYE, *author of 30 Days with 30 Saints*

why worry?

A CATHOLIC'S GUIDE TO LEARNING
to let go

JEFF DUNN

**TWENTY-THIRD
PUBLICATIONS**
twentythirdpublications.com

TWENTY-THIRD PUBLICATIONS
1 Montauk Avenue, Suite 200, New London, CT 06320
(860) 437-3012 » (800) 321-0411
www.twentythirdrdpublications.com

ISBN: 978-1-62785-151-0
Library of Congress Catalog Card Number: 2015957222
Printed in the U.S.A.

CONTENTS

INTRODUCTION

Hello, my name is Jeff. I am a chronic worrier.

Hello, Jeff.

I come from a long line of worriers. A grandmother who was always worrying about whatever family member wasn't in the room at the time. Aunts who worried when my cousins and I would go outside to play. My mom even worries when she doesn't have anything to worry about. She thinks something must be really wrong for her not to have anxiety. Really. I'm not making this up.

Worrying comes naturally to me. I worry about the

usual things: my job, my health, my retirement account. I worry when I gain weight that I won't be accepted by those who have perfect bodies. As a matter of fact, a good deal of my worry is that I won't be accepted by, well, anyone.

My wife.

My children.

My friends.

My coworkers.

Those I see at church.

Those I sit next to at a baseball game.

Those who are driving behind me in traffic.

The other day I announced to those in line behind me at the grocery that I really did have only twenty items in the speedy checkout lane. I was worried that these people wouldn't like me—people I had never seen before and will most likely never see again. I was afraid they would think I had sneaked an extra item onto the conveyer belt. This is how bad I am.

I worry about unusual things, too, like, will we ever send humans safely to Mars? Will drinking milk that expired yesterday make me sick? What happens if I drop my cell phone in the toilet?

I get anxious on Sunday nights thinking of work the next day. What if I don't do a good job this week? What if I get fired or laid off—how will I provide for my family? My anxieties grow throughout the week. It's Wednesday, and I still have work in my inbox from Monday. It's Thursday, and I'm not as prepared for my meeting as I should be. It's Friday, and now I have to face a weekend feeling guilty because I didn't work hard enough to warrant two days of relaxation.

It's Saturday, and my anxiety reaches a fever pitch as I look at my yard and see that it's not as neat and trim as those around me. I look around the inside of my house and see piles of half-started, never completed projects. I begin to look forward to Mass, only to realize that it's Saturday, which means confession. What if I don't do a good job at confession? What will my priest think of me? What if he thinks I'm wasting his time?

Then it's Sunday again, and I look back and see I've wasted an entire week worrying and being anxious, and I have little to no hope of this next week being any different.

To quote St. Paul, "Wretched man that I am! Who will deliver me from this body of death?" *(Romans 7:24)*.

Anxiety paralyzes me. I get an email, and I'm not sure of the best way to answer it. So I let it sit while I "consider" the best way to respond. And the more I consider, the more afraid I get of saying the wrong thing. So I never answer it. I don't return calls. I don't answer texts. I hide in the perceived safety of my own fear. It's my version of the infant game: If I can't see you, then you can't see me to reject me.

I worry about the future. The future of my career, my possessions, my garden. I'm anxious about our country and those we have chosen to run it for us. I'm fearful about the economy. I'm worried about where Catholicism is headed in the next generation and all of the people leaving the church.

I'm worried. I'm scared. I'm anxious. I'm fearful.

I don't want to be, but I don't know how to stop. I have sought medical help, and that has brought some temporary relief. I have gone to counselors, who again have been of some help. Others offer little to no help. When I've talked to men I respect in the church about my anxieties, most often I feel like I've just admitted I have leprosy and am contagious. Or they will say, "But you're always so upbeat. How could you be anxious?"

I want to be free from fear and worry and anxiety. I want to live in the peace and joy and freedom Jesus promised to us, but I can't seem to find firm footing to walk that out. So I thought that perhaps, just maybe, if I talk this out with you, I would find some way to navigate through the jungle of worry. And I thought that, perhaps, you too would find a hand to hold as we walk together in the darkness of depression and doubt and fear.

I'm not promising you an easy journey. Sorry, but there are no "Five Easy Steps" to easing anxiety. There is no surefire cure for worry. Everyone is going to have to find their own path. Perhaps, however, if we talk this out together, we'll begin to see some light in the darkness.

Maybe you have picked up this book simply to find help for common, everyday worry. The kind of worry that nags at you but does not paralyze you. Let's walk together and hear what the Scriptures and saints say about worry. Let's encourage each other as we grow in faith and trust in our Father who cares for us. There is a way to live without the constant buzz of worry in our ears.

Then again, maybe you are like I am at times—completely overcome with anxiety to the point you cannot function properly. You may have generalized anxiety disorder, a condition that can be diagnosed and treated by medical professionals. What I am going to discuss in this book can still be of help to you, for we know God uses all sorts of methods for our healing, including physical (medicines and physical therapy), emotional (counseling) and spiritual (prayer and meditation).

We all worry at some level. Thus, it is to all of us that Jesus says, *"Do not let your hearts be troubled."* Now, let's see how we can follow him in this.

1

WORRY
DEFINED

~~~~~~~~~

Let not your hearts be troubled, neither let them be afraid.
JOHN 14:27

These words of Jesus are familiar, especially to those whose hearts and minds are constantly troubled and afraid. There is an implicit message here, one that is, in a strange kind of way, encouraging. If Jesus says not to worry, then he knows that we are troubled and fearful creatures. And he knows that, left to ourselves, we can no more avoid fearful hearts than we can swim from California to Hawaii. He is not telling us to lift ourselves up by our own emotional bootstraps. He is saying that there is a way out of a life of worry, and it is found through him. And that is comforting. Yet many of us think Jesus' words can't apply to us today, that our worries are more than he can handle.

We humans are world-class worriers. If worrying was an Olympic sport, we would take gold medals in the 100-meter worry, 400-meter anxiety, and 1600-meter life paralysis. Christian storyteller Max Lucado shares the tale of a man who was always worrying about everything in his life. He worried so much that he couldn't do anything else. So he made up his mind to hire someone to do his worrying for him. He hired a man to be his designated worrier for the sum of $200,000 a year. His first day on the job arrived, and the designated worrier thanked his new boss for the opportunity he was given, but then asked, "Where are you going to get $200,000?"

His boss said, "That's your worry."

We spend a lot of time worrying. A lot of time. Benenden Health in Great Britain conducted a survey regarding stress and found that we worry on average:

14.3 hours a week
744 hours a year
45,243 hours in a lifetime
1,885 days in a lifetime

This means that the average person spends more than five years of his or her life worrying. Think about that.

We could each earn a college degree in that amount of time. Instead, we are graduates of Fear U., with a degree in Worry, Anxiety, and Fret.

In 2014, an outbreak of the deadly Ebola virus hit several African nations. Nine people who, unknown to them at the time, had contracted the disease traveled to the United States where it was determined they had Ebola. Two more people, both nurses in a Texas hospital, were diagnosed with the virus after caring for the Ebola patients. Of all of these cases, two people died of the Ebola in the U.S. But that didn't stop the fear from paralyzing the country and dominating the news for weeks on end. A town in Maine learned that one of their teachers went to a conference in Dallas while a hospital in that city treated an Ebola victim. When the teacher returned to Maine, she was told not to report to her school for twenty-one days—the incubation period for the virus—even though she had not been closer than ten miles to the hospital in Dallas. Fear won out over facts.

Likewise, a smallpox outbreak occurred in New York City in 1947. The mayor ordered everyone in the city to be vaccinated against the disease, causing mass fear and confusion as volunteers went door to door urging residents to get their shots. Famed author and public speaker Dale Carnegie relates the experience from his perspective.

> More than two thousand doctors and nurses worked feverishly day and night, vaccinating crowds. The cause of all this excitement? Eight people in New York City had smallpox and two had died. Two deaths out of a population of almost eight million. Now, I have lived in New York for over thirty-seven years, and no one has ever yet rung my doorbell to warn me against the emotional sickness of worry—an illness that, during the last thirty-seven years, has caused ten thousand times more damage than smallpox.

Anxiety, fear, and worry are at an epidemic level in our world today. And, just as in 1947, we need to ring doorbells to warn people of the danger of this emotional sickness.

BUYING FEAR

We have made fear the most valuable emotion in the world. Look at any advertisement on TV, or online, or in a newspaper or magazine. What is being presented is not a product or service, but the fear you should have of being without that product or service. Fear of looking overweight, of not being popular, or of being left out. Fear of dying, fear of being broke, fear of your teeth not being shiny white.

Fear of not having enough.

Author S. Yates wrote a very practical book for those planning to walk the Camino de Santiago in Spain, a popular pilgrimage path. In *Pilgrim Tips & Packing List Camino de Santiago*, Yates gives the two reasons why pilgrims carry too much with them: "Fear and insecurity, and the marketing that takes advantage of them, are the main reasons why pilgrims carry far too much on the Camino." She continues, "Fear and insecurity develop not only out of lack of information, but also from false information. Here is where marketing raises its ugly head. For a product to sell there has to be a demand for it, and, if there is no demand, you have to create one artificially."

We have allowed ourselves to become fearful by what we watch, read, and listen to. All of the voices in our lives trying to sell us something have made us afraid of not having everything, or at least not having as much as we can.

We live in constant fear of not having enough, yet we also fear what we consume. There seems to be a new report each week to tell us the dangers of eating food our grandparents ate with gratitude. Are these reports shared for our health benefits, or to get us to buy some alternative that is billed as safe? Michael Pollan, author of *The Omnivore's Dilemma*, says, "It is very much in the interest of the food industry to exacerbate our anxieties about what to eat, the better to then assuage them with new products."

We line up to buy what fear is selling. Jesus saw this, and thus made his bold statement to his followers: "Let not your hearts be troubled, neither let them be afraid" (*John 14:27*).

Jesus knows that fear, worry, and anxiety have had a strong grip on men and women since the beginning of time. It stems from an act committed by our first parents, Adam and Eve, in the Garden of Eden. God the Father had made everything good for them—food to eat, comfortable shelter, companionship with each other as well as with the Father. Everything they needed or wanted was there for them. All God denied them was eating from the tree of knowledge of good and evil.

"What is good and what is evil is for me to know," he said. "If you eat of this tree, you will be trying to assume what is not for you. You will be trying to be godlike in your knowledge. Instead, trust me to know what is good and what isn't, and then you can live in peace."

The temptation, however, proved too great. The idea of being like God in knowing if something was good or bad overcame their trust in God. They ate of the fruit of the tree of the knowledge of good and evil, and thus was born a lifetime of worry, fear, mistrust, and anxiety. We fear being out of control of our future. We are anxious that we might lose what we think we own. We worry about something that might happen, and thus cannot deal with where we currently are. Worry projects into the unknown future, while God wants us to live in the now. We still taste the fruit of the knowledge of good and evil. But what we call good, God may see is harmful for us; and what we think is evil, the Lord may see is ultimately for our good.

Thomas Merton struggled with the anxiety brought on by the knowledge of good and evil in his life. He sought relief from his anxieties, but they didn't come as he would have wanted. In his classic autobiography *The Seven Storey Mountain*, Merton said he heard God speak these words to him:

> Everything that touches you shall burn you, and you will draw your hand away in pain, until you have withdrawn yourself from all things. Then you will be all alone....
>
> Every created joy will only come to you as pain, and you will die to all joy and be left alone. All the good things that other people love and desire and seek will come to you, but only as murderers to cut you off from the world and its occupations....
>
> You will have gifts, and they will break you with their burden. You will have pleasures of prayer, and they will sicken you and you will fly from them.
>
> And when you have been praised a little and loved a little I will take away all your gifts and

all your love and all your praise and you will be
utterly forgotten and abandoned and you will
be nothing, a dead thing, a rejection. And in that
day you shall begin to possess the solitude you
have so long desired. And your solitude will bear
immense fruit in the souls of men you will never
see on earth.

Do not ask when it will be or where it will be or
how it will be: On a mountain or in a prison, in a
desert or in a concentration camp or in a hospital
or at Gethsemani. It does not matter. So do not ask
me, because I am not going to tell you. You will
not know until you are in it.

If you heard the Lord speak these words to you, would
they encourage you to trust him more, or to become anxious at what lies ahead? Somehow, Merton used this to
strengthen his faith in God, and did enter into a lifetime
of solitude. And his solitude has borne much fruit in the
souls of those whom he never met on earth.

Jesus, of course, knew the condition of the human
race from the beginning. He came with a great an-
nouncement—The kingdom of heaven is here, now—
and we are all invited in. The kingdom of heaven is the
Garden of Eden restored. Yet we can only enter in by
trusting the Lord to lead our lives, not by our continuing
to eat of the tree that was forbidden us. And when we

enter into the kingdom of heaven, we can enjoy the gift Jesus has given us: Peace.

> Peace I leave with you; my peace I give to you. Not as the world gives do I give to you. Let not your hearts be troubled, neither let them be afraid.
> (JOHN 14:27)

That is what this little book is about. This book is not about clinical depression, which needs medical help to overcome; it is about the everyday worry and anxiety that seek to rob our souls of life little by little, the "death by a thousand small cuts." It is about the journey from worry, fear, and anxiety to the peace of God, peace that is stronger than anything that would cause our hearts to be troubled or afraid. We will see what God thinks of anxiety in his creation. We will journey with saints who struggled with worry and fear. And we will find comfort in prayers that encourage and comfort us in our times of anxiety.

WHAT IS WORRY?

Anxiety is a feeling of worry and fear that goes beyond our current situation or condition. It is a projection of what *might* happen and whether what *might* happen would be good or bad. Worry, one person has said, is a waste of the imagination. It is our mind painting a picture of what will never come.

Worry is also a shield we hold up to keep others from seeing us as we truly are. To let others know our "real self" is dangerous indeed. We don't want to be seen as frauds or as the failures we believe ourselves to be (again, this stems from us trying to know what is good and bad in our lives). Our fear is that we might be known for who we really are, and our "real self" is not someone we have yet come to love.

Merriam-Webster defines worry as a verb meaning "to think about problems or fears; to feel or show fear and concern because you think that something bad has happened or could happen." That is a lot of thinking.

If we look at the word's origins, we are taken back to Old German, where the root of our word for worry, *wurgen,* means "to strangle." That seems very appropriate to our discussion of worry and anxiety. It is a feeling, coming from our imagination, that strangles us, leaving us paralyzed, unable to deal with real life, life in the now.

This, of course, is not how God designed us to live. Let's look at how our Creator sees worry.

ST. PAUL THE APOSTLE

W hen we read the Bible, we must be careful not to project images on the writers and others we read about that aren't true. After all, they are men and women just as we are. St. Paul the Apostle is credited with writing more than half of the New Testament, yet he was not immune from worries and fears. We read his words in his second letter to the church at Corinth.

> We do not want you to be unaware, brothers and sisters, of the affliction we experienced in Asia; for we were so utterly, unbearably crushed that we despaired of life itself. (**2 CORINTHIANS 1:8, NRSVCE**)

This is how many with constant fears and worries would describe their lives—unbearably crushed, despairing of life itself. Yet Paul did not remain in this state. We read just few chapters further in this same epistle,

> We are afflicted in every way, but not crushed;
> perplexed, but not driven to despair; persecuted,
> but not forsaken; struck down, but not destroyed.
> (2 CORINTHIANS 4:8,9, NRSVCE)

What helped Paul to change his perspective? I think it can be explained in two other passages.

> Indeed, we felt that we had received the sentence
> of death so that we would rely not on ourselves
> but on God who raises the dead.
> (2 CORINTHIANS 1:9, NRSVCE)

> But this precious treasure—this light and power
> that now shine within us—is held in a perishable
> container, that is, in our weak bodies. Everyone
> can see that the glorious power within must be
> from God and is not our own. (2 CORINTHIANS 4:7,
> THE LIVING BIBLE)

In these two passages, we see that Paul is not relying on his own strength or power to overcome despair. He relies entirely on the power of God to raise him from the death of his fears and worries.

We can seek St. Paul's help in our struggle with anxiety, knowing he knows just how we are feeling.

*St. Paul, glorious martyr for the sake of Christ,
we ask your intercession in our time of fear and
worry. We, like you, are crushed on all sides by
anxiety in our lives. We despair of life itself. Pray
for us, St. Paul, that we, like you, may not rely
on our own strength but on the power of God
alone who can raise us from our death. Amen.*

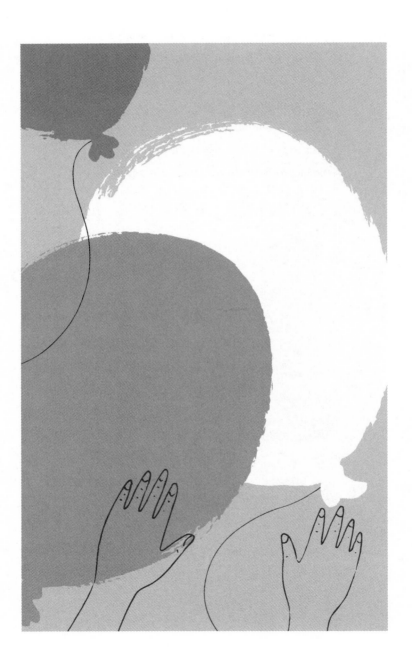

2

Getting Back
to the Garden

~~~eeelleeee~~~

Imagine yourself working at a job that is fun, challenging, and rewarding. You work outside in a tropical paradise with your loving mate by your side. Each evening after work, you and your employer, who is also your best friend, go for a long walk in the cool shade of the trees, talking about what you have been learning and doing on your job, listening to his stories and wise advice. There are no time clocks to punch, no annual reviews, and no taxes to file. Your housing and food needs are wonderfully met. What more could you want?

Then one day, a disgruntled employee of your boss comes to you and says, "So, do you want to know the secrets of the boss's success? Do you want to know what he has been keeping from you? Come with me—let's hack into his computer and see what is really going on. Then you can break away from that slave driver and be your own boss."

You do as he suggests. You hack into your boss's computer and see how he operates his enterprise, both the good and the bad aspects. But you are found out. The boss calls you into his office, and you are ashamed to stand before him as you now are. He tells you that you are fired from your job. You'll have to give up your home, and you will be responsible for your own keep from now on. And perhaps worst of all, no more walks in the evening with your best friend.

Yes, you now know more than you did; you are streetwise and have some business acumen, but you've lost your home and your friend. Instead of loving your work and having all of your needs generously met, you're on your own to scratch out a hard living. And instead of being able to confide in your best friend, you are now afraid of him and hide when he comes around.

This is a picture of what happened when our ancestors Adam and Eve disobeyed God and ate of the tree of the knowledge of good and evil in the Garden of Eden. Perhaps now we can see how we humans began to be worriers. It all began when we lifted a load we were not mean to bear. We were meant to live in peace, not to be consumed with cares and concerns about what to do next. Yet it was our choice. We wanted to know what it would be like to be the boss. Now that we are, we are constantly thinking about what we need to do next, while hounded by what we did wrong yesterday and what might go wrong tomorrow. Work is hard and hardly rewarding. What we make today goes to pay for what we bought yesterday and what we will need to buy tomorrow. It seemingly never ends until we die. And then our sons and daughters inherit what we have not completed and keep the cycle going.

The question before us is: Now what?

BEING AN ARTIST

The answer requires us all to become artists. Stick with me now, ok?

It is said that all good art answers four questions:

Who are we?
Why are we here?
What has gone wrong?
How do we get back?

Joni Mitchell addresses this in her song "Woodstock" when she sings, "We've got to get ourselves back to the garden." That is our goal—to get back to the carefree paradise God meant for us to inhabit. We all long for

work that is fulfilling, a place to live that is safe and comfortable, enough to eat and drink, and clothes to wear.
Most of all, we desire that close relationship with God
that was lost due to our disobedience. To achieve that,
let's each of us mix our paints, pick up a brush, and create some art.

Who are we? We are the children of the Creator of the
Universe, whom he individually crafted in the wombs
of our mothers.

You are not an accident. You were lovingly crafted
by God himself to be uniquely you. And God cares so
much for you as you are that he knows the exact number
of hairs on your head.

For a long time, I thought I was part of the group plan.
The Bible says, "For God so loved the world…." I figured I
was part of the world, so God just kind of got stuck with
me. It has been a long, sometimes hard process to get to
where I knew I was loved by my Creator individually. You
too are a handcrafted masterpiece by the Master Artist.

Why are we here? We are here to know and be known
by our Creator.

The question of why we are here is enough to keep
all of the philosophers of the world busy until the end of
time. Perhaps it would help to think of life, the universe,
and everything as a play. God is the writer and director

of the play, and all of the angels and demons, all of the stars and planets and moons and comets are the audience. You and I and all who have come before us and all who will follow us are the actors. The title of the play is Immense Love. It came about one day when God was trying to explain to a group of angels the concept of love freely chosen and freely given. When they still weren't getting what he was telling them, he said, "Here, let me show you what I mean by unconditional love."

In this great play, we are not given lines to memorize. We can ad-lib our own lines, something the director calls "free will." And in this play, we find that the director climbs out of his chair and steps onto the stage as one of the actors. He puts on the performance of a lifetime, and shows us all just what immense love looks like. At the conclusion of the play, he invites us all to the cast party that will last for all eternity.

What has gone wrong? We wanted to run the show instead of trusting our care to our Creator. As we already saw, we decided we wanted to run the Garden instead of trusting the owner to know what is best. We were kicked out and now live hand-to-mouth as we scratch out a hard life by our own strength.

How do we get back? There is only one way to get back to the Garden, and that way was given by Jesus Christ,

God's only Son. He said we must repent and believe. That is the gate we walk through to return to paradise. The good news is this: the gate to the Garden of Eden is once again open to us. Jesus invites us into the Garden, called the kingdom of heaven. All is forgiven. We are free to return to where we were meant to be all the while.

Once we have considered these four steps, we are ready to paint a picture. The world is our canvas, and in it we create the work of art known as our life. What does all of this talk of being an artist have to do with worry? Well, fear and worry will keep us from even making the first brush stroke. Or we will resort to a paint-by-number kit that is safe and predictable, where if we follow all of the rules, we won't ever make a mistake and no one will criticize us. But it is not art, and it's not the picture God wants from us.

If we want to get back to the Garden, if we want to create a grand painting with our lives, we must learn to get past fear and worry and doubt. We must cast off the lines that we think make us safe and learn to sail on the great sea of God's mercy and grace. This is not easy. It takes a lifetime and then some. But oh! is it worth it.

ST. DYMPHNA

The traditional story of St. Dymphna has her born in Ireland in the seventh century to King Damon. When Damon's wife died, he searched his kingdom for another woman who was as beautiful as his wife. Finding no one, in the madness of his grief he turned his attention to his daughter. Dymphna had taken a vow of chastity for the Lord, and upon learning her father intended to have her as his wife, fled Ireland for the mainland of Europe. She settled in the Belgium town of Geel with her confessor/priest, Father Gerebernus.

Damon eventually tracked them down and, with his daughter refusing to become his wife, had them both beheaded. The townspeople in Geel buried them first in a cave, then moved them to a church built in honor of Dymphna. Soon, the town was overrun by those with anxiety and fear coming to be healed of their emotional distress.

Whether or not the story of Dymphna is accurate as portrayed, what continues to this day in Geel is very true, and nothing short of a miracle. Those suffering from mental illnesses flock to Geel, where they are taken in by the townsfolk and treated as members of the community as they seek healing. Some come and stay for a few months, some for years, some for the rest of their lives. They are not seen as strange or abnormal, but as brothers and sisters in need of God's touch in their lives.

St. Dymphna is known as the patron saint for those with anxiety issues. If that is you, and you cannot make it to Geel in Belgium, you can call up St. Dymphna for her help. Here is a prayer to St. Dymphna:

> *Glorious St. Dymphna, you are the patron of the anxious and emotionally disturbed. I know that through the circumstances of your life you can relate to those who are fearful, anxious and confused. I turn to you, dear virgin and martyr, sure of your willingness to take my worries into your hands. I praise and bless the Lord for giving you to us as our helper in time of need. I trust that through your kind intercession He will restore my peace of mind and give me a calm spirit.*

Pray for me, St. Dymphna, that my anxiety and emotional turmoil may end, and that I may again know the peace that passes all understanding. Amen.

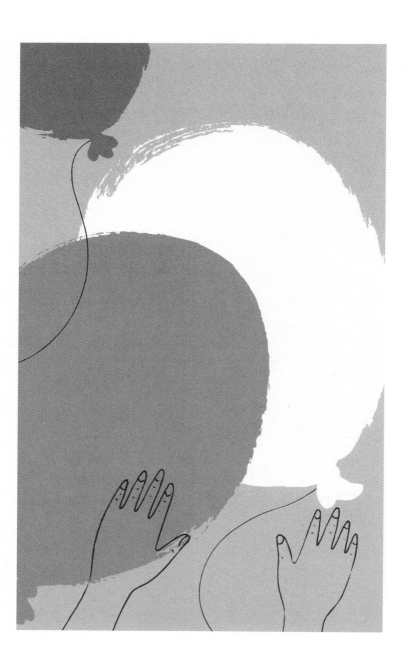

3

THE CURSE
OF WORRY

～～ℓℓℓℓℓℓ～～

"Therefore I tell you, do not worry about your
life, what you will eat or what you will drink, or
about your body, what you will wear. Is not
life more than food, and the body more than
clothing? Look at the birds of the air; they neither
sow nor reap nor gather into barns, and yet your
heavenly Father feeds them. Are you not of more
value than they? And can any of you by worrying
add a single hour to your span of life? And why
do you worry about clothing? Consider the lilies
of the field, how they grow; they neither toil nor
spin, yet I tell you, even Solomon in all his glory

was not clothed like one of these. But if God so
clothes the grass of the field, which is alive today
and tomorrow is thrown into the oven, will he
not much more clothe you—you of little faith?
Therefore do not worry, saying, 'What will we
eat?' or 'What will we drink?' or 'What will we
wear?' For it is the Gentiles who strive for all these
things; and indeed your heavenly Father knows
that you need all these things. But strive first for
the kingdom of God and his righteousness, and
all these things will be given to you as well.

"So do not worry about tomorrow, for
tomorrow will bring worries of its own.
Today's trouble is enough for today."
(MATTHEW 6:25–34, NRSVCE)

Why do you think Jesus spent so much time talking
about worry? Was it to make us feel guilty when we worry? Or was it to show us that there is a better way to live?

Jesus addressed common, everyday worry with his
disciples in the Gospel of Matthew. Just as today, people in the time of the first disciples worried about putting food on the table and having something to wear.
Jesus asked them why they were concerned about these
things, pointing out that birds don't hold a job or have
savings accounts, yet they are fed abundantly. And then
he pointed to flowers in the field around him, and said

these were clothed beautifully, even though they didn't have charge accounts at any department store. "If my Father is going to take care of birds and flowers," he said, "don't you think he is going to take care of you?"

Yet to this day we persist in worrying about what we don't have, or worrying that what we have isn't enough. Jesus saw that worry causes us to not trust God, and this is why he was so adamant with his disciples that we are to cease from cares and burdens. He was, in essence, saying, "Look, the things you need will be taken care of by your Father in heaven today and every day. So don't focus on these things."

So what does Jesus want us to do if not care for today? The opposite of worry, as Jesus taught in this passage from Matthew, is faith. Faith believes *God Is*. Faith believes *God Can*. Faith believes *God Will*. The writer of the New Testament Letter to the Hebrews tells us the importance of faith in the life of the believer: "And without faith it is impossible to please God, for whoever would approach him must believe that he exists and that he rewards those who seek him" *(Hebrews 11:6)*.

So in order to please God, we must trust him, put our faith in him. And we can't trust God and worry at the same time. One of them must win out. Faith in God is hard. After all, we can't see God, but we can see our troubles right before us. No wonder we so often default to worry over faith.

What does worry get us? According to Jesus, worrying won't add even an inch to our height. When we worry, we are telling God we can't trust him. Think about this. Each time we receive the Eucharist, we are proclaiming that we trust the sacrifice of Jesus on the cross to be sufficient for our sins and to be the gateway into the kingdom of God. Then we leave the church and begin to worry that we don't have enough in our lives—enough money, enough health, enough love. How can we believe God is able to save our souls but not provide for our earthly needs? If God can't get us through today with enough to eat and drink, how can we believe he is capable of getting us safely to heaven?

When you are anxious, you let your circumstances rule you. Nowhere in Scripture or church teaching do we ever hear that we won't have difficulties in this life. On the contrary, the Bible clearly tells us that part of our experience in this life will be facing problems.

> Man that is born of woman is of few days and full of trouble. (JOB 14:1)

> For all their days are full of pain, and their work is a vexation; even at night their minds do not rest. This also is vanity. (ECCLESIASTES 2:23)

> [Jesus said to his disciples,] "I have said this to

you, so that in me you may have peace. In the
world you face persecution. But take courage; I
have conquered the world!" (JOHN 16:33)

We are not to judge one another's difficulties. What
might be simply an obstacle to one may be a paralyzing challenge to another. The point is we will all face
problems in our lives. Worrying about them causes us to
focus on the circumstances. Faith in God gets our eyes
off of the problems and on the one who gives us peace
even in the midst of the storm.

In the Old Testament book of 2 Chronicles, chapter 20, we read the story of the fourth king of Judah,
Jehoshaphat. A messenger came to the king with some
very sobering news. A great army was marching toward
Judah intent on destroying the entire country. This army
was far more than what Judah could even begin to think
of defeating on its own. King Jehoshaphat cried out to
God, "O our God, will you not execute judgment upon
them? For we are powerless against this great multitude
that is coming against us. We do not know what to do,
but our eyes are on you."

The Spirit of God came upon a prophet by the name
of Jahaziel, who proclaimed, "Listen, all Judah and in-
habitants of Jerusalem, and King Jehoshaphat: Thus says
the LORD to you: 'Do not fear or be dismayed at this great
multitude; for the battle is not yours but God's. This

battle is not for you to fight; take your position, stand still, and see the victory of the LORD on your behalf, O Judah and Jerusalem.' Do not fear or be dismayed; tomorrow go out against them, and the LORD will be with you."

Of course this goes against our natural inclination. When we are faced with a problem, most of us will roll up our sleeves and work our best to solve the problem. If faced with an overwhelming army bent on destroying us, very few would say, "The best thing to do is just to stand still." Yet that is what the Lord asked the people of Judah to do. After this command, it would have been wrong for them to do anything else, including worry about what was going to happen. "For the battle is not yours, but God's."

Worry is a curse that brings nothing but trouble into our lives. Worry is us trying to take control of our own lives, decide good from bad on our own, and solve our problems with our own strength. Instead of crying out, "We do not know what to do, but our eyes are on you," most of us will say, "If it is to be, it's up to me." And that is the heart of all sin.

Now that we have seen that worry is something God does not intend for our lives, just what can we do about it?

ST. PADRE PIO

The twentieth-century Italian saint known as Padre Pio is perhaps best remembered for his stigmata and other miracles associated with him. Yet he spent much of his time as a much-sought-after spiritual director. Padre Pio had five rules for personal spiritual growth.

Daily communion
Weekly confession
Spiritual reading
Meditation
Examination of conscience

He summed all of this up within his life's motto: "Pray, hope, and don't worry." He continued this thought, saying, "Worry is useless. God is merciful and will hear your prayers."

Padre Pio recognized that much of our worry comes from trying to take on burdens we were not meant to carry. He said, "The habit of asking 'Why?' has ruined the world." He counseled his spiritual pupils to let go of the need to understand why and instead to trust God completely.

We would do well to take Padre Pio's "Pray, hope, and don't worry" as our motto as well.

....

"It is our work to cast care, and it is God's work to take care."

≫ **THOMAS WATSON** ≪
THE ART OF DIVINE
CONTENTMENT

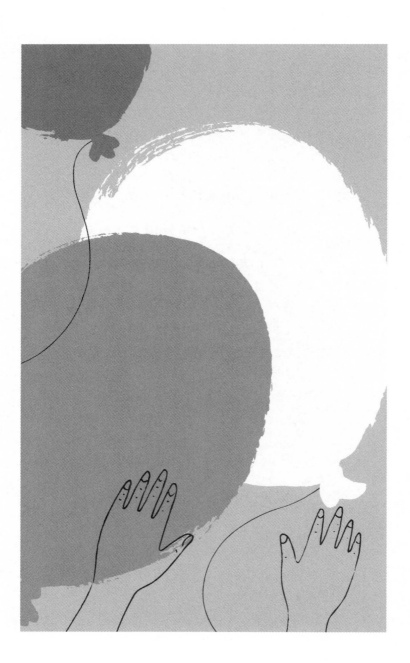

4

THINGS THAT DON'T WORK

⟟⟟⟟⟟ ℓℓ ⟟⟟⟟⟟

Pickles.

A survey conducted by researchers at the College of William and Mary found a correlation between eating fermented foods, such as pickles and sauerkraut, and lowered anxiety. Maybe that has been our problem all along—the lack of pickles in our diet. Could we really defeat our anxieties just by eating more dills, bread and butters, and sweet gherkins?

Somehow I don't think it is that easy.

We have looked at how worry affects us, both as individuals and as a community. We have seen how anxiety first came to be a part of our lives. And we know we need to get back to the Garden where fear and anxiety fade into the shadows. We all want to learn to not worry, to live abundantly in the mercy and grace of our Lord. How do we get to that point? Before we look at ways to help us to stop worrying, let's first look at ways that will not help.

YOU CAN'T USE ACCOUNTING PRINCIPLES TO CONQUER FEAR.

Have you ever had anyone tell you to just "count your blessings"? You know: "How can you worry when you have so many good things going in your life? If you count your blessings, you'll see you have more good things than bad in your life." I had a friend say that to me when I told him I was struggling with anxieties. It didn't help.

In accounting, you want to balance your income with your outgo. It is important that we don't spend more than we make. Yet when it comes to our emotions, "one for one" doesn't work. Yes, if you were to list your blessings next to things you are worried about, you would probably see that you have many more things to be thankful for than to be anxious about. But life is not like a balance sheet. You might be the most "blessed" person alive, and yet just one worried thought can overwhelm you.

It's always good to be thankful, and we all have many

blessings in our lives. Scripture does tell us, after all, that we are to not forget all of God's benefits (see Psalm 103). It would seem rational that counting up more good things in our lives than bad things would tip the scale in favor of happiness. Yet real life says that is not the way things work. Anxieties are not rational. Fear can cloud good times like a pop-up thunderstorm. We need something more than a calculator to drive out worry.

WEARING A "HAPPY" MASK WILL NOT MAKE YOUR WORRIES GO AWAY.

I remember one time asking two friends, both evangelical pastors, to pray for me regarding my anxieties that had led to depression. They both looked shocked that I would ask that. "How could you be depressed?" asked one of my friends. "You are the most positive person I know." He hesitated in praying for me because he thought I must be joking about being depressed. I assured him I was very much in need of prayer and of help, but he was hard to convince. I wore a "happy face" mask everywhere I went, so people thought I was totally carefree. Yet I saw the real me. I knew that if the mask would come off, I would look as if I were carrying the weight of the world.

Masks provide distance and a perception of safety (more on safety in a minute), but that can backfire. When you are ready to remove the mask so you can receive help with your anxieties, you may not be recognized.

Remember the song, "Don't Worry—Be Happy"? (I'm sorry if that song is now stuck in your head!) It was a catchy tune, and it would be a great motto for life—if it were only true. Many books have been written to say all we have to do to shake the blues is to think happy thoughts. Yes, thinking happy thoughts may have helped the Darling children in *Peter Pan* to fly, but for us, real life tends to overwhelm even the happiest thoughts we can muster.

TRY TO REMAIN IN A SAFE PLACE.
This would seem to be the most sensible thing we could do. After all, what kind of person runs outside during a storm? Fools tempt God by purposely plunging into danger just for the thrill of it.

Yet it is just as foolish to try to live a life of complete safety in this world. When I was in college, I had a poster on my wall with a picture of a sailboat out at sea. Under the boat were these words: *A ship in a harbor is safe, but that is not what ships are built for.* My roommate couldn't understand this saying. "If a ship is safe in a harbor, why doesn't it stay there?" he asked. "If that is the case," I said, "why build the ship in the first place?"

Jesus was in a boat with his disciples when a terrific storm arose. These men were fishermen, accustomed to dealing with wind and waves, yet this storm was particularly fierce, so much so that they feared for their lives.

When they turned to Jesus, they found him asleep in the boat! Why wasn't he helping them? Why didn't he get them to a safe place? When their worries finally got the better of them, they cried out, "Don't you care about us? We're going to drown!" Jesus, waking from his sleep, stood up and calmed the storm with his words. Then he turned to the disciples and said, "Why do you have such little faith?" Where was their safety? It was being with Jesus, the Master of wind and waves, no matter where Jesus was.

The psalmist captures this picture in Psalm 107 *(NRSV)*.

Some went down to the sea in ships,
    doing business on the mighty waters;
they saw the deeds of the LORD,
    his wondrous works in the deep.
For he commanded and raised the stormy wind,
    which lifted up the waves of the sea.
They mounted up to heaven, they went down to the
    depths;
    their courage melted away in their calamity;
they reeled and staggered like drunkards,
    and were at their wits' end.
Then they cried to the LORD in their trouble,
    and he brought them out from their distress;
he made the storm be still,

and the waves of the sea were hushed.
Then they were glad because they had quiet,
   and he brought them to their desired haven.
Let them thank the Lord for his steadfast love,
   for his wonderful works to humankind.
Let them extol him in the congregation of the people,
   and praise him in the assembly of the elders.

Now, what can we do to overcome worry?

JULIAN OF NORWICH

J ulian was an anchoress—setting aside her life to live in a small "cell" in consecration to the Lord—in the late fourteenth, early fifteenth century in England. In her desire to know Christ in a greater way, she requested three things from the Lord:

A greater understanding of Jesus' passion;

A sickness close to death while she was young, so that she could experience all that a body and soul experienced in death without actually dying;

Three "wounds": absolute contrition, kind compassion, and steadfast longing for God.

Julian's prayer was answered, and she became so sick that a priest was summoned to administer the last rites. As she lay apparently dying, she received fifteen "showings," or revelations. Then, surprising everyone including herself, Julian recovered. She wrote down her revelations (the first known book to be written by a woman in the English language), including this from her thirteenth "showing":

In my folly, before this time I often wondered
why, by the great foreseeing wisdom of God,
the onset of sin was not prevented: for then, I
thought, all should have been well. This impulse
[of thought] was much to be avoided, but
nevertheless I mourned and sorrowed because of
it, without reason and discretion.

But Jesus, who in this vision informed me of all
that is needed by me, answered with these words
and said: "It was necessary that there should be
sin; **but all shall be well, and all shall be well,
and all manner of thing shall be well.**"

These words were said most tenderly, showing
no manner of blame to me nor to any who shall
be saved.

It is the phrase, "all shall be well, and all shall be well,
and all manner of thing shall be well" that has resound-
ed in the hearts of those who chronically worry, making
Julian a good companion in times of stress and anxiety.

....

*"Be not miserable
about what may
happen tomorrow.
The same everlasting
Father, who cares
for you today,
will care for you
tomorrow."*

» **FRANCIS DE SALES** «

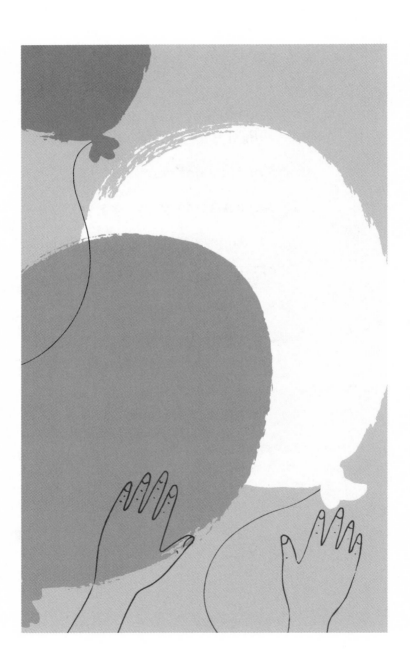

5

SWIMMING YOUR WAY OUT OF ANXIETY

Don't worry. That was the command Jesus gave to his followers, and, thus, to us.

If you want to make it sound more "biblified," it would read, *Let not your hearts be troubled.* Since we are commanded not to worry, it must be possible for us to corral our fears and anxieties and keep them in check. Just how do we go about doing this?

First of all, however, a question.

Do you want to stop worrying?

Impertinent? I don't think so. Some people become

so wedded to their worries, they would fear not having a personality apart from worrying. There are those who love the attention they get as they "bravely carry on in spite of the many burdens of life." You may know people like that. Perhaps this describes you. Worry gets us noticed. It gets us sympathy. If you were to stop worrying, you might just become an average person without the extra attention you get now.

So let me ask you again: Do you want to stop worrying? Are you willing to give up the attention your fears and anxieties garner you? Being without worry may make you a bit more anonymous. Is that ok with you?

If so, then one or more of the following may help you to reduce your anxieties.

TAKE AN INVENTORY

Examine your life as closely as you can, with pen and paper handy, and list those things you *can* control: what time you wake up, the food you eat for breakfast, how you get to work, what time you take your breaks, what you do for entertainment after work, what time you go to bed.

These are just a few of the many things in your life where you have a choice. Keep digging. List as many as you can think of. Then turn the paper over, and list all of the things in your life you have no control over. The weather. Traffic jams. The stock market. What your coworkers think of you. What your neighbors think of you. What your family thinks of you. Whether or not the vending machine at work will have any Peanut M&Ms when it's time for your break. Keep listing the things you have no control over. Use more paper if you need to.

Now, look again at what you *do* control in your life. Are there any of the items you need to move to the back of the paper? If you listed, "I'm in control of other people's reactions to me," cross that off. So many of our worries come from thinking we are in control of what is never in our hands, like what others think of us. You want to know a secret? You wouldn't worry so much about what others think of you if you realized how little they do.

Why would you insist on being anxious about that which is not yours to carry, whether it be the tree your neighbor is planting in her yard or a ruling by the Supreme Court? Perhaps a story will help us see what is ours to carry and what isn't.

STORYTIME

A man went to work for a good but stern landowner. The landowner gave him a task.

"I want you to move this rock up to the top of that hill. Put it in the wheelbarrow, keep going steadily, and you will soon reach the top and be able to release your burden."

At first the worker did just as he was shown. He loaded the rock—which was too heavy to be carried, but easy to move with the wheelbarrow—and began to push it uphill. As he was going up the path, a friend came to him and asked him a favor.

"I see you are taking that rock up to the top of the hill. Would you mind if I put my rock in your wheelbarrow as well? It really won't be that much more work for you, and it would save me so much time." So the worker agreed and loaded his friend's rock in with his master's. This made the cart a bit harder to push, but after all, he was helping a friend.

Next he passed by the schoolhouse. The teacher came out and said, "Just in time! I was about to have my students each carry their rocks up the hill, but now I see you have room to carry them. You won't mind, will you? They are much smaller than the two rocks you have in there now." And the pupils came out in single file and put their rocks one after another into the cart. After the schoolhouse he passed a cottage where a man and his wife were each holding their rocks. "You'll help us, won't you? As you can see, my wife is pregnant and it would be very hard for us to get up the hill."

Now the man's cart was very heavy indeed. He struggled mightily to go each yard, yet he knew what his master expected of him. The final place he passed on his way was the church.

"Oh!" said the pastor as he emerged with a very large

rock. "I had just been praying for help with my rock, and now I see God has answered me. Please take this rock to the top of the hill with all of the others. I will be praying for you, my son."

Night came, then daylight, then night again, yet he was not even close to the top of the hill. He fought to push his cart inch-by-inch, fearing it would soon collapse under the weight of the load he was pushing. His master, expecting him to have returned by now, went in search of him. When the master found the worker on the third day, loaded down with rocks and not yet at the crest of the hill, he was very angry.

"What are you doing with all of those rocks?" he demanded. "I told you to take my rock. If you had done the job as I gave it to you, you would have been to the top and back again two days ago. Now you are too weary to get any of these rocks to the top."

What rocks are you carrying in your cart that your Master has not given you to carry? Anything that is out of your control—which is more than you probably imagine—is someone else's rock that is weighing down your cart. Yes, carrying one another's burdens is Scriptural, and it does make us look heroic to be helping others, even in the midst of our struggles. But if this causes us to stumble in what the Lord has given us to do, we won't get our rock or anyone else's to the top of the hill.

FIX WHAT YOU CAN

Take another look at your paper, the side where you listed the things you can control. Which of these things are
causing you anxiety? For instance, let's say you are barely
getting to work in time each morning. Certainly that
might cause you to be stressed. But this is something you
can fix. Set your alarm for fifteen minutes earlier than
you usually get up. Or plan a different route for your
drive to your job. How many things on your list of what
you control can you adjust to make things easier for you?

"And next you'll be telling me that water is wet."

Ok, I know it seems common sense to fix what you
can. Yet for many of us, it is the simple, seemingly easy
tasks we don't do. While we are looking for a magic pill
that will take away all of our worries, the things we can
do go undone. It is easier to be a nervous wreck driving
to work in the mornings than it is to set the alarm clock
a bit earlier. "God helps those who help themselves"
sounds nice, but it isn't biblical, nor does it reflect the
nature of God. (Much closer to the truth is "God helps
those who cannot help themselves.") Yet why would the
Lord come to our aid to help us to stop worrying if we
are unwilling to take some simple steps?

Are you worried about putting on extra weight? Then
don't have that second helping of dessert. Are you afraid
you won't have enough money to get you through the
end of the month? Perhaps you shouldn't go out to eat

but rather eat what is in your cupboard at home. I know when my wife and I were struggling to make ends meet financially, we decided we could live without cable TV and a newspaper subscription. That extra hundred dollars a month made a positive difference, and the world as we knew it didn't end just because I didn't have a morning paper or five hundred channels of nothing to scan.

It also helped to feel like I was doing what I could to control my anxiety, even if I knew that in the bigger picture, all was in God's hands.

HOW MUCH IS ENOUGH?

Money, and what money can buy us, is a constant element of our worries. As Mark Twain said, "The *lack* of money is the root of all evil." Somehow we have allowed ourselves to be convinced that having more money will solve our problems. But as Gregory Jeffrey puts forth in his book *Why Enough Is Never Enough*, having peace about our finances means to be at peace in trusting God. According to Jeffrey, there are those who have very little, yet who are satisfied, and those who comparatively have much, yet live in anxiety and worry that what they have is not enough. Obviously, there is not a magic amount of money that will cure all of our fears. John D. Rockefeller, the great oilman of the depression era, was asked how much money would be enough.

The millionaire answered, "Just a little bit more."

Are you worried because you don't feel you have enough money? Take an honest look at what you have. What do you consider "enough"? It does no good to compare yourself to others. There will always be those who are worse off than you as well as those who have much more than you will ever have. Only you know how much you need, how much you desire.

Many books have been written and sermons preached on money and our relationship to it. I'm not going to go into detail here other than to say that Jesus recognized the power money has over us. He said we can't serve both money and God—sooner or later we will have to choose one over the other. The tension inherent in that choice is what leads to so many of our fears and worries. It is in our best interest to choose quickly who we are going to serve. I'm not saying it is easy to trust the Lord when the bills are piling up, when there is more month left than money, when you don't have enough to get you to your next paycheck. I live there myself. And to be very honest, my first reaction is seldom to trust the Lord for his provision. I first look to myself. Should I try to get another job? Do I have anything I can sell for some quick cash? Maybe I should take money out of my IRA. It's then that my wife will kindly say, "Why don't we pray about this?" You would think that after more than four decades of walking as a follower of Jesus, that would be the obvious solution. Obvious to others, yes, but not to me. Apparently, I'm still in the Garden, reaching for the fruit of the tree of the knowledge of good and evil, still wanting to be in control of my own life, still wanting to come up with my own solutions.

Instead, I should remember how the Lord cared for the children of Israel as they circled around in the wilderness for forty years. He gave them fresh manna to eat each day. There was always enough for that day. If, however, they tried to gather more than they needed and hoard it, it would spoil and be unfit to consume. What does this tell us? Jesus reminds us of this when, in the prayer he taught his disciples, he says we are to ask the Father for our daily bread. It is not helpful to worry about tomorrow's provisions. We are to gather today's manna, and know that tomorrow there will be a fresh batch waiting for us.

BREATHE

Anxiety can take a dreadful toll on our bodies. One way to combat this is with purposeful breathing. When you feel anxiety coming on, take in a deep breath through your nose. Breathe it all the way down. You should feel your abdomen tighten as you do this. Hold it for a couple of seconds; then slowly let it out from your mouth. The more exaggerated you make this, the more helpful it will be. Of course, now you'll worry what others are thinking of you. Let them think what they will. These deep, cleansing breaths will help ease your anxieties.

Many times people will experience tightness in their chest when they are panicking. It can feel like having a heart attack, but in reality it is tightness from shallow, chest-only breathing. That is why it's important to slow down, exhale deeply, then practice belly, or diaphragmatic, breathing. If you do this correctly, you will feel a bit of a strain in your abdomen, like you've been doing sit-ups. It is helpful to practice this type of breathing when you are not in an anxious state so that it can be more natural to you when you are anxious and in need of cleansing breath.

You might say there is nothing more natural than breathing, and you would be right. But most of our breathing is shallow, chest-breathing. What you want to practice is breathing that doesn't come naturally. If you are not familiar with this style of breathing, it is going to seem strange to you at first. Try taking it step by step.

Exhale through your mouth. Let out a good, loud sigh to get out as much wind as you can.

Now, breathing in through your nose, push your belly out. This will allow oxygen to get deep into your lungs.

Hold your breath for as long as you like. This isn't a contest, and you don't want to start feeling faint. Two to three seconds is probably enough.

Exhale again through your mouth.

Repeat this whole process four or five times, then rest.

Not only will you be getting oxygen deep into your

lungs and blood vessels, but as you do this exercise, you'll be thinking about your breathing and not what is causing you anxiety. Perhaps that is the greatest benefit from deep breathing. And there is a spiritual benefit in this as well. The word used often in the Bible to refer to the Spirit of God is "breath." God breathed into the dust to create the first people. Jesus breathed on his disciples to impart to them the Holy Spirit. As you practice deep, cleansing breaths, meditate on how the Spirit of the Creator of the universe lives in you.

LAUGH A LOT

Q: Why are elephants so wrinkled?

A: Have you ever tried to iron one?

Ok, ok. Maybe that elicited a groan from you rather than a guffaw. (Elephant jokes used to be all the rage.) But the truth is that laughter really is a good medicine. We read in the Old Testament that "a cheerful heart is a good medicine, but a downcast spirit dries up the bones" *(Proverbs 17:22)*. Sometimes all it takes to shake us from our worries is a good, long laugh.

There is plenty of evidence that laughter acts as medicine.

When we laugh, we draw in deep draughts of oxygen for our heart and lungs. The ripple effect is felt in other organs in the body, and we begin to feel "normal" again.

It releases endorphins, the body's natural way to fight

stress. Endorphins also improve our immune system, regulate our appetite, and release sexual hormones.

Laughter can stimulate blood circulation, which relaxes muscles that may have tightened up in times of stress. A good, hearty laugh can leave you feeling relaxed for up to an hour afterward.

Studies have even shown that regular laughter can help prevent heart disease, which would mean one less thing to worry about.

So where do you find sources of laughter? Some will find it in books, others in movies or TV shows. I have found that watching reruns of *Frasier* (my all-time favorite TV show) just before bed helps me to have a more refreshing sleep. I laugh with the show, and go to bed without the stress of the day weighing me down.

The best use of laughter is to maintain what the Bible calls a "merry heart." Take all of life as a show put on to make us smile. There is something in everyone we meet to make us smile, something in most every circumstance to make us chuckle, if only we take time to look.

In the world of Harry Potter, there exist Boggarts, dark blobs that take the shape of the thing the person who encounters the Boggart is most afraid of. Just as my fears look different from your fears, my Boggart will be different from yours. The way to chase away Boggarts, however, is the same for everyone. The spell you cast is call *riddikulus*. This causes the Boggart to change into the form of something you find laughable, and Boggarts cannot stand to be laughed at. They flee from laughter as darkness flees when a light is shone.

Even if you are not a fan of Hogwarts or Harry Potter, you can appreciate that the word *riddikulus* is a takeoff of the English word ridiculous. And our word comes from two Latin words, *ridiculum* (meaning "joke") and *ridere* ("to laugh"). Fear flees laughter, for it is brought into the light and shown to be nothing more than a great "what if," a Boggart, rather than a substantive object or situation we must deal with. Laughter, therefore, is not just good for your body, but for your soul as well. In the face of laughter, the demons of fear and worry run and hide.

BE WHERE YOU ARE

Dale Carnegie in his classic book *How To Stop Worrying And Start Living* tells the story of an industrialist near the turn of the twentieth century who took a transatlantic ride on a large ship. While he expected that there would be large rooms for people to gather, and large holds for the cargo, he was surprised to find instead a series of smaller rooms, all of which could be sealed of from each other. The captain explained to the industrialist that this was so the ship could remain watertight in case of an emergency. If one room somehow became flooded, it could be sealed off from the rest of the ship so they could continue sailing.

This taught the man that each person also has many rooms. There are rooms filled with past experiences, successes and failures, and rooms filled with plans for the future, each with its own set of cares and concerns. By sealing off each of these rooms from his mind, he saw he could live in the present without being flooded by the past or the future. This concept became a central focus of Carnegie as he sought to teach people how to live free from worry. Today the concept is a major part of what is referred to as "mindfulness," a method of meditation where you focus on your thoughts, emotions, and environment at that moment. It's also called "living in the moment."

Jesus told his disciples, "Do not worry about tomorrow; tomorrow will take care of itself" *(Matthew 6:34, NABRE)*. Eugene Peterson, in his translation of the Bible, *The Message,* puts it this way:

> Give your entire attention to what God is doing right now, and don't get worked up about what may or may not happen tomorrow. God will help you deal with whatever hard things come up when the time comes.

That sounds like living in the moment to me. How does this help you to relieve your worries? If you seal off the past and the future and only look at today, you have shut off at least two thirds of your worries. I'm not saying this is easy—not at all. It takes practice. Start with the breathing exercise mentioned at the beginning of this chapter. Listen to the sounds around you as you breathe. Focus on inhaling. Focus on exhaling. Live in the moment with your breathing. If you can do this for a minute the first time out, that's great. Begin to do this as often as you can. Pretty soon you will find it becomes a habit. A worrying thought will creep into your mind, but instead of entertaining it, you focus on taking five belly breaths, listening to the air going in and coming out. When you are done, you may be surprised to find the anxious thought moved on.

TAKE A HIKE

Recent studies seem to show that those who spend even a few minutes in nature have lower levels of stress than those who keep to their cubicles. We know that walking is good for our health, but where we walk affects our attitudes.

Being out in nature, whether in a deep forest or under the shade of a tree in your backyard, somehow acts to keep us from focusing on our problems and their causes. Compulsively paying attention to what is wrong in our lives is called "rumination." It is on the other end of the anxiety scale from worry: Rumination draws our attention to what has gone wrong in the past, while worry focuses us on what might go wrong in the future. Neither is good for us; together they serve as a vice that squeezes joy from us.

Perhaps one way that taking a walk in a natural environment helps us battle rumination is that we see that the mountains and hills, the trees and the rocks around us, have been there a very long time and have endured many trials. That twisted trunk of the mighty oak shows how it survived a great wind. The crevice in the rocky side of a mountain shows us that even though it was split during an earthquake, the mountain did not fall. Even the weeds and wildflowers on the side of the trail show how a delicate seed, once it had fallen into the ground, transformed, took root, and became what we see today.

If we can begin to look at the wind and earthquakes of our past not as disasters but as God's means for making us into who he wants us to be, then we can neutralize the grip rumination has on us, if even just for the short time we are walking under the sky or a canopy of trees.

WRANGLE YOUR THOUGHTS

Finally, beloved, whatever is true, whatever is
honorable, whatever is just, whatever is pure,
whatever is pleasing, whatever is commendable,

if there is any excellence and if there is anything
worthy of praise, think about these things.

(**PHILIPPIANS 4:8, NRSV**)

The Apostle Paul wrote these words to the church in
Philippi, people who had reason to worry. Persecution
of Christians was on the rise, there were famines in the
region, and Paul, their spiritual father, was in prison. Yet
Paul instructs them to not worry about anything, but pray
about everything. And then he gives them this practical
advice: think on good things.

We know that fears and worries are simply thoughts
that plague our minds. If we are to get them out of our
thoughts, we need to be ready to replace them with other, healthy thoughts. Believe me, this does not come easily. It takes a lot of practice to push one thing out of your
mind and put another in its place. This does not mean
we are to live a Pollyanna life where we never face anything difficult or discouraging or ugly. Paul is saying we
are not to live there in our thoughts, that we are to bring
our minds into submission to us and make them focus
on the good. And what is good according to St. Paul?

He starts with what is true. We know that worries
about tomorrow aren't true – they can't be, as tomorrow
has yet to arrive. And we also know that truth is not a
concept or an idea, truth is a Person. Jesus told his disciples, "I am the way, and the truth and the life" (*John*

14:6). So in thinking on what is true, we are focusing our mind's attention on Jesus.

We go on from there to think on what is honorable, just, pure. This may mean cutting back on what we read in the news—much that is anything but honorable, just, or pure. It may mean cutting out some movies or TV shows we watch or books we read. You know the saying—Garbage In, Garbage Out. In this case, the garbage we put into our minds produces garbage that comes out in the form of fears that we don't measure up to the looks of people on the screen or worries that we don't have enough like the "successful" people we read about. If honor, justice, and purity are to be our goals, we are going to need to stop feeding jealousy and pride in our minds.

Paul finishes up his list by saying we are to think on what is pleasing, commendable, excellent, and worthy of praise. Who are we seeking to please in our thoughts? We must have our aim to be to please God in all we do, in all we say, and in all we think. Our fears and worries don't please him for, as we have seen, these cause us to not trust God but trust in our own abilities. Our fears and worries stem from our eating from the one tree in the Garden that was forbidden us. Thinking as Paul directs us to think helps to get us back where we belong.

BROTHER LAWRENCE

Nicolas Herman was born in France in 1614. Impoverished from birth, Herman joined the army in order to survive. He retired from the military after being wounded in battle, worked for a time as a valet, and then had an encounter with the Lord where he saw that God really did love him. He eventually joined the Discalced Carmelite priory in Paris as a lay brother, taking the name Lawrence of the Resurrection.

Brother Lawrence lacked education and experience to do more than the most menial tasks within the priory. His wound caused him to struggle in physical activities, and he felt, as he said, "clumsy." Yet he did not let his lack of abilities hinder his devotion to God. He purposed to "practice God's presence" at all times, and to do all for the love of God. In doing so, Brother Lawrence kept his anxieties from overcoming him. In the Age of Enlightenment when many wrote of the power of human reason, one of the most enduring books came from a simple man who felt he had little to offer. *The Practice of the Presence of God* has stayed in print for more than four hundred years and is a source of comfort and encouragement to Catholics and Protestants alike.

Here are some of Brother Lawrence's insights from that book.

> Along with this total abandonment must go a complete acceptance of God's will with equanimity and resignation. No matter what troubles and ills come our way, they are to be willingly and indeed joyously endured since they come from God, and God knows what he is doing.
>
> The difficulties of life do not have to be unbearable. It is the way we look at them—through faith or unbelief—that makes them seem so. We must be convinced that our Father is full of love for us and that he only permits trials to come our way for our own good.
>
> That we ought to give ourselves up to GOD, with regard both to things temporal and spiritual, and seek our satisfaction only in the fulfilling of his will, whether he lead us by suffering or by consolation, for all would be equal to a soul truly resigned.

God knoweth best what is needful for us, and all that he does is for our good. If we knew how much he loves us, we should always be ready to receive equally and with indifference from his hand the sweet and the bitter: all would please that came from Him. The sorest afflictions never appear intolerable, except when we see them in the wrong light.

6

Learning to Float

꿍꿍꿍꿍

The exercises and techniques mentioned in the previous chapter are all very helpful for one struggling to overcome anxiety and worry. The problem with them is this: they can all be done without relying on the Lord. And that is what got us into this mess in the first place.

Remember, worry stems from when we, through our ancestral parents Adam and Eve, decided we wanted to be like God and know good from evil. What was never meant for us to carry now bends us very low indeed. We are not going to be able to get out from under this load on our own. What I want to suggest in this chapter will go against what most of us have ever learned. It may sound simple and easy, but in reality it is quite hard to learn to do.

First, however, I want to revisit worry—just what is worry, anyway? We have talked about worry as a cause of emotional and bodily illnesses, a force that occupies our minds and keeps us from thinking creatively and productively. We even traced worry's beginnings to the original sin. Worry is paying today for things that may never happen tomorrow. Worry is all of this.

Most of all, however, worry is a lie.

Worry lies about knowing what will happen in the future.

Worry lies about the effects of your past.

Worry lies about what others think of you.

Worry lies and tells you that you will always be the way you are today.

Worry lies and wants you to believe you don't have enough.

Worry lies and makes you believe you don't do enough.

Worry lies and tells you that you will never be free from worry.

Worry, in short, lies.

Worry works like this. We experience some uncomfortable action or thought, and immediately worry lies to us to tell us we are in danger. Our ancestors relied on the sense of danger to stay alive. "There's a bear—I need to run!" Or, "There's my enemy—I need to fight." This is where the "fight or flight" mentality began, and for many, it was a proper response to real danger. But in our culture today, we face far fewer real dangers. Very few of us will ever see a bear outside of a zoo, and most of us don't have enemies who are threatening us with bodily harm. But we still have the fight or flight thing going on inside. So when the thought "There's my neighbor. What will she think of me getting my paper in my robe and slippers at noon? She's going to think me lazy and worthless" comes into our minds, we want to either fight by yelling, "It's not what you think! I've been working really hard in my house today!" or fly by running back into our house, hoping the neighbor didn't see us. Then the anxious thoughts build throughout the day to the point we never again want to see our neighbor. "I'll just sell my house and move to another state!"

Seriously, we let worry lie to us and cause us to run or duke it out over the dumbest things at times. Let's go back to what I mentioned in the introduction. I was in the express lane at the grocery store. I had counted the items in my cart, and sure enough I only had twenty, which the sign over the register said was the maximum amount for that lane. As soon as I started unloading my items onto the conveyer belt, three people got in line behind me. Each one had only one item. And each person was eyeing me as if I were buying a month's worth of groceries. Worry started lying to me: "They are all mad at you. They're going to complain to the manager. And that big guy holding the huge package of toilet paper, the one with the squinty eyes and tattoos everywhere, is going to follow you out to the parking lot and…" So I decided to fight. I turned around and said, "Really, I only have twenty items!"

The three people in line behind me glanced at me, glanced at my items, and then looked away. I had won the fight! Just for good measure, I also chose flight as a response, and hoofed it out of the store as quickly as I could after paying.

I bought worry's lie and reacted just as it wanted me to.

I could have taken a quick inventory of my wheelbarrow and seen that I had just piled in a rock that wasn't mine to carry. I could have tried to fix things on my own, such as asking the clerk to stop ringing up my order to let the three people behind me go first. I could have practiced my belly breathing (though the likelihood of hyperventilating right then was very high). Maybe I should have laughed out loud or asked myself, WWFD? (What Would Frasier Do?)

None of these things, good as they may be, would have really helped me right then. What I needed was to learn to float.

LEARNING TO FLOAT

Swimming instructors will tell you that even for advanced swimmers, learning how to float can be very difficult. Fr. Thomas Green, the author of *When the Well Runs Dry*, tells of living in the Philippines and trying to teach Filipinos, who grew up knowing how to swim, to float in the water. "When we do have a picnic and I try to teach these people of the sea how to float, it is puzzling to see what a difficult art floating really is—difficult not because it demands much skill, but because it demands much letting go," writes Green. "The secret of floating is in learning not to do all the things we instinctively want to do. We want to keep ourselves rigid, ready to save ourselves the moment a big wave comes along—and yet the more rigid we are the more likely we are to be swamped by the waves; if we relax in the water we can be carried up and down by the rolling sea and never be swamped."

Swimmers have goals; floaters allow the current to take them wherever it will. Swimmers are in control of their actions; floaters let go of their actions.

Swimmers put forth effort to get from one place to another; floaters just, well, float.

Dr. Claire Weekes applied this idea of floating to dealing with anxiety. Weekes was an Australian doctor who helped many people learn to work through anxiety through her clinics and her books. Weekes discovered that doing things to try to reduce or eliminate worry actually makes things worse. When we try to fight anxiety, it is like throwing gasoline on a fire. And when we try to run from our anxiety, we find our anxiety can outrun us every time. So she came up with a new approach. She called it floating. Instead of running from our anxiety, or using techniques to fight it, we need to lay our head back and float through it.

When we put forth our own efforts to fight anxiety, we are actually fanning the flames of the fire we want to put out. We are calling attention to what we want to go away. Our efforts to fight anxiety actually make it worse. It is paradoxical to think that the best way to overcome worry is to just let it be, but that really is true. Do you remember those little bamboo finger tricks we had as kids? You would put one index finger in one end, and your other index finger in the other end. Now, try to take it off. Your first instinct was to pull your fingers out, right? But the harder you pulled, the tighter it became. The way to get it off was to relax your fingers and push them together—just the opposite of what we would do naturally.

Worry is the same way. The harder you pull on it, the more power you give it to bind you, to keep you ensnared in its trap. To overcome worry, you need to stop pulling. You need to stop fueling anxiety with your efforts. You need to float.

The psalmist lifts up this cry of the Lord when he

writes, "Be still, and know that I am God!" *(Psalm 46:10, NRSV)*. Other translations put the "Be still" in more direct words.

"Let go of your concerns" (*God's Word*)
"Stop fighting" (*Good News Translation*)
"Stand silent" (*Living Bible*)
"Step out of the traffic" (*The Message*)
"Stop your striving" (*New English Translation*)
"Be calm" (*The Voice*)

What all of these translations of this familiar passage have in common is a call for us to stop our efforts and trust God. Again, let's remember the only way we can please God is by trusting him. And trusting God goes against how we think we are to act. As Fr. Green writes, "The problem is we must decide whether we want to swim or float."

> Most of us want to do a little of both. When we tire of swimming we like to float, but when our floating carries us beyond the safe zone, then we swim again to get back where we are secure. It seems, however, that we cannot do both together forever. The whole experience of the dark night or the cloud of unknowing appears to be the Lord's ways of trying to make floaters out of swimmers.

He, it seems, definitely wishes us to float. He
wants us to have as our goal our total surrender
to the flow of this tide. He has another goal, it is
true. He is leading us somewhere; our floating
is not to be an endless, directionless circling in
a fathomless sea. But that is *his* goal; he would
like us to trust him enough to relax, to leave the
goal wholly to him, and to concretize our trust by
savoring fully the expanse of sky and sea which
is open to our gaze now. Only those who are
totally secure in their love can live thus fully the
present moment. Only those who have forgotten
themselves completely, who truly float free, can
give their whole voice to blessing the wind and
the wave. (**WHEN THE WELL RUNS DRY, P. 146**)

We are God's masterpiece in the making, even if all we
see right now are a jumble of mismatched pieces, or
splatters of paint on a canvas, or a tangle of threads on
the back of the tapestry. If we want to have a hand in this
work of art, we need to go back to the four questions all
artists must answer.

Who are we? We are broken, messed-up people living in
a broken, messed-up world who are learning to come to
grips with the idea that God's love for us surpasses what
we could ever imagine.

Why are we here? We're here so that we can be put on display before all the angels and saints as a way for God to show his glory, his boundless and unconditional love.

What went wrong? We grasped what was not ours to have. We took upon ourselves the responsibility of knowing right from wrong, good from evil, instead of simply living as God designed us to. In doing this, we brought anxiety and worry into our lives.

How can we get back? We must let go of the striving and trust God. We must learn to float instead of swim.

It is the simplest thing in the world, and it is the hardest thing we will ever do.

7

GOD CAN

~~~~llee~~~

So here we are. We are all in the same boat, we worriers. And our boat is being driven by the fierce wind in a direction we didn't choose, and it is being swamped to the point of sinking by the enormous waves. And where is Jesus? He's napping in the stern of the boat, the place where the helmsman would sit, the person who was responsible to steer the boat in the right direction and ensure its safe arrival at its destination.

How does that make you feel? Honestly, how do you feel when all in your life is a royal mess and it seems that Jesus is sound asleep? You go to Mass, you pray the Rosary, you pray your novenas, you recite the Divine Chaplet every day at three o'clock sharp. Yet Jesus sleeps on. If you're doing all the right things, why aren't you being rescued?

So you take the psalmist's advice and you become still. You stop your striving, step out of the traffic, and stay calm. You practice floating instead of swimming. And as you are floating, you are drawn to the edge of a waterfall. What more can you do?

I have one final idea for you. One that is practical and is backed by Scripture. It will require you to get a box, some packing tape, a pair of scissors, some paper, and a pen. How big a box? For most people, a shoebox will do. Others with large worries may need a hat box. Still others, with huge worries facing them, will want to get a refrigerator box. You will have to decide how big your box should be.

Once you have a box, seal it up with packing tape. Use a lot to seal it so you can't get into the box easily. Now, using your scissors, cut a slit in the top big enough to insert small pieces of paper. How are you doing? On the top of the box, write in large letters "God Can."

GOD CAN

On a piece of paper, write down what is worrying you the most right now. You may want to start it by writing, "I can't _____."

I can't seem to lose weight. Will my spouse/partner still accept me?

I can't meet my sales goals this month. Am I going to get fired?

I can't stay focused in school. Am I going to fail my class?

I can't get my children to behave. Am I a bad parent?

I can't put money in the savings account. What happens when I go to retire?

I can't stop sinning. Does God still love me?

Each time you start to worry, write it down and put it in your box. And as you slide that paper in the slot, read what is written there.

God can.

You can't, but God can. In doing this, you are practicing what Scripture tells us to do: "Cast all your anxiety on him, for he cares for you" *(1 Peter 5:7, NRSV).*

When you write down what is worrying you and put it in the box, you have released your problem to the Lord. You can't, but he can. You are giving him your anxiety in a practical way. You see the paper falling into the box, and because the box is sealed, you can't get it back. Let it go. Let your worry rest now in the hand of the Lord. He cares for you—that is why you can cast your anxiety on him. There is nothing too big for our God to handle, and nothing too small for him to notice.

Worry and fret will dog us all our lives. I don't think we will ever, this side of heaven, get to where we don't ever worry or experience anxiety. It is what we do with these feelings when they invade our lives that matters. We have looked at some practical and biblical methods for dealing with our fears and worries. Now, it's up to you to decide what to do. Will you continue to anxiously swim in your fears and worries, or will you trust God enough to let go of your anxieties and know that he can take care of them?

Then next step is up to you.

Prayers
for Worriers

The Merton Prayer
from *Thoughts in Solitude*

*My Lord God, I have no idea where I am going.
I do not see the road ahead of me. I cannot
know for certain where it will end. Nor do I
really know myself, and the fact that I think
I am following your will does not mean that
I am actually doing so. But I believe that the
desire to please you does in fact please you.
And I hope I have that desire in all that I am
doing. I hope that I will never do anything
apart from that desire. And I know that if
I do this you will lead me by the right road,
though I may know nothing about it. Therefore
I will trust you always though I may seem
to be lost and in the shadow of death. I will
not fear, for you are ever with me, and you
will never leave me to face my perils alone.*

St. Thérèse of Liseux Prayer
from *Story of A Soul*

May today there be peace within.
May you trust God that you are exactly
    where you are meant to be.
May you not forget the infinite possibilities
    that are born of faith.
May you use those gifts that you have received,
    and pass on the love that has been
        given to you.
May you be content knowing you are
    a child of God.
Let this presence settle into your bones,
and allow your soul the freedom to sing, dance,
    praise, and love.
It is there for each and every one of us.

The Serenity Prayer

God grant me the serenity
to accept the things I cannot change;
courage to change the things I can;
and wisdom to know the difference.
Living one day at a time;
Enjoying one moment at a time;
Accepting hardships as the pathway to peace;
Taking, as he did, this sinful world
as it is, not as I would have it;
Trusting that he will make all things right
if I surrender to his will;
That I may be reasonably happy in this life
and supremely happy with him
forever in the next.
Amen.

Prayer for Decision Making

*Gracious God, it's time. It's time to make
the hard decisions. Sometimes I'm scared,
sometimes I'm confused, and sometimes I just
don't want to believe I have to make a decision.
Help me to trust you. Give me strength and
wisdom so that whatever happens honors my
loved ones and you. Thank you for hearing me
and answering my prayer.*

Amen.

A Prayer to Heal Stress

*Heavenly Father, please grant me peace of
mind and calm my troubled heart. My soul is
like a turbulent sea. I can't seem to find my
balance, so I stumble and worry constantly.
Give me the strength and clarity of mind to
find my purpose and walk the path you've
laid out for me. I trust your love, God, and
know that you will heal this stress. Just as the
sun rises each day against the dark of night,
please bring me clarity with the light of God.
Amen.*

Thoughts
on Worrying

"Historians will probably call our era 'the age of anxiety.'
Anxiety is the natural result when our hopes are
centered in anything short of God and his will for us."

BILLY GRAHAM

"Worry is a dividend paid to disaster before it is due."

IAN FLEMING

"Worry is a weighty monster with poisoned tentacles. It
clutches at us, grabs at our minds, steals our breath, our will.
It lurks. It pounces. It colors how we perceive the world."

MARY E. DEMUTH, *Everything: What You Give
and What You Gain to Become Like Jesus*

"I am an old man and have known a great many
troubles, but most of them have never happened."

MARK TWAIN

"It's a waste of time worrying about something that worry won't fix; it's about as useful as trying to feed your pet rock."
RICHELLE E. GOODRICH, *Smile Anyway: Quotes,*
Verse, & Grumblings for Every Day of the Year

....

"Earthly goods deceive the human heart into believing that they give it security and freedom from worry. But in truth, they are what cause anxiety."
DIETRICH BONHOEFFER

....

"Worrying is carrying tomorrow's load with today's strength—carrying two days at once. It is moving into tomorrow ahead of time.
CORRIE TEN BOOM

....

"If you trade your authenticity for safety, you may experience the following: anxiety, depression, eating disorders, addiction, rage, blame, resentment, and inexplicable grief."
BRENÉ BROWN

"Our anxiety does not come from thinking about
the future, but from wanting to control it."
KHALIL GIBRAN

....

"Our anxiety does not empty tomorrow of its sorrows, but
only empties today of its strengths."
CHARLES H. SPURGEON

....

"Do not let your peace depend on the words of men.
Their thinking well or badly of you does not make you
different from what you are. Where are true peace
and glory? Are they not in Me? He who neither cares to
please men nor fears to displease them will enjoy great
peace, for all unrest and distraction of the senses arise
out of disorderly love and vain fear."
THOMAS À KEMPIS, *The Imitation of Christ*

....

"The beginning of anxiety is the end of faith, and
the beginning of true faith is the end of anxiety."
GEORGE MULLER

"Anxiety is not only a pain which we must
ask God to assuage but also a weakness
we must ask Him to pardon; for He's told us
to take no care for the morrow."

C.S. LEWIS

....

"We imagine that a little anxiety and worry is an indication
of how wise we really are; it may be an indication of how
wicked we really are."

OSWALD CHAMBERS, *God's Workmanship*

....

"Good morning! This is God. I will be handling
all of your problems today. I don't need your
help at all, so have a nice day!"

(Sign in a worker's cubicle seen at a Christian college)

....

"Worry is most often a prideful way of thinking
that you have more control over life and its
circumstances than you actually do."

JUNE HUNT

"Excessive caution destroys the soul and the
heart, because living is an act of courage, and
an act of courage is always an act of love."

PAULO COELHO, *Manuscript Found in Accra*

....

"But here we see the peace of God is not the absence of
negative thoughts, it is the presence of God himself."

TIM KELLER

....

"Sometimes, too often, I don't want to muster
the energy. Stress and anxiety seem easier."

ANN VOSKAMP, *One Thousand Gifts:*
A Dare to Live Fully Right Where You Are

Trust in the Lord!

The Lord is my strength and my might,
and he has become my salvation.

EXODUS 15:2

....

Be strong and bold; have no fear or dread...
because it is the Lord your God who goes with you;
he will not fail you or forsake you.

DEUTERONOMY 31:6

....

I keep the Lord always before me;
because he is at my right hand, I shall not be moved.

PSALM 16:8

....

Guard me as the apple of the eye;
hide me in the shadow of your wings,

PSALM 17:8

Even though I walk through the darkest valley,
I fear no evil;
for you are with me;
your rod and your staff—
they comfort me.

PSALM 23:4

Be still, and know that I am God!

PSALM 46:10

Cast your burden on the Lord,
and he will sustain you.

PSALM 55:22

When I am afraid,
I put my trust in you.

PSALM 56:3

My flesh and my heart may fail,
but God is the strength of my heart and my portion forever.

PSALM 73:26

God will cover you with his pinions,
and under his wings you will find refuge;
his faithfulness is a shield and buckler.

PSALM 91:4

....

When I thought, "My foot is slipping,"
your steadfast love, O Lord, held me up.
When the cares of my heart are many,
your consolations cheer my soul.

PSALM 94:18–19

....

They are not afraid of evil tidings;
their hearts are firm, secure in the Lord.

PSALM 112:7

....

I lift up my eyes to the hills—
from where will my help come?
My help comes from the Lord,
who made heaven and earth.

PSALM 121:1–2

Where can I flee from your presence?
If I ascend to heaven, you are there;
if I make my bed in Sheol, you are there.
If I take the wings of the morning
and settle at the farthest limits of the sea,
even there your hand shall lead me,
and your right hand shall hold me fast.
If I say, "Surely the darkness shall cover me,
and the light around me become night,"
even the darkness is not dark to you;
the night is as bright as the day,
for darkness is as light to you.

PSALM 139:7–12

Trust in the Lord with all your heart.

PROVERBS 3:5

But now thus says the Lord,
he who created you, O Jacob,
he who formed you, O Israel:
Do not fear, for I have redeemed you;
I have called you by name, you are mine.
When you pass through the waters, I will be with you;
and through the rivers, they shall not overwhelm you;
when you walk through fire you shall not be burned,
and the flame shall not consume you.
For I am the Lord your God,
the Holy One of Israel, your Savior.

ISAIAH 43:1–3

For surely I know the plans I have for you,
says the Lord, plans for your welfare and not
for harm, to give you a future with hope.

JEREMIAH 29:11

Jesus said "Therefore I tell you, do not worry about your life, what you will eat or what you will drink, or about your body, what you will wear. Is not life more than food, and the body more than clothing? Look at the birds of the air; they neither sow nor reap nor gather into barns, and yet your heavenly Father feeds them. Are you not of more value than they? And can any of you by worrying add a single hour to your span of life? And why do you worry about clothing? Consider the lilies of the field, how they grow; they neither toil nor spin, yet I tell you, even Solomon in all his glory was not clothed like one of these. But if God so clothes the grass of the field, which is alive today and tomorrow is thrown into the oven, will he not much more clothe you—you of little faith? Therefore do not worry, saying, 'What will we eat?' or 'What will we drink?' or 'What will we wear?' For it is the Gentiles who strive for all these things; and indeed your heavenly Father knows that you need all these things. But strive first for the kingdom of God and his righteousness, and all these things will be given to you as well. So do not worry about tomorrow, for tomorrow will bring worries of its own. Today's trouble is enough for today."

MATTHEW 6:25–34 (SEE ALSO LUKE 12:24–34.)

"Come to me, all you that are weary and are carrying
heavy burdens, and I will give you rest. Take my yoke
upon you, and learn from me; for I am gentle and
humble in heart, and you will find rest for your souls.
For my yoke is easy, and my burden is light."

MATTHEW 11:28–30

They went to him and woke him up, shouting,
"Master, Master, we are perishing!" And he
woke up and rebuked the wind and the raging
waves; they ceased, and there was a calm.

LUKE 8:24

"Do not let your hearts be troubled. Believe in God,
believe also in me. Peace I leave with you; my peace I give
to you. I do not give to you as the world gives. Do not let
your hearts be troubled, and do not let them be afraid."

JOHN 14:1, 27